DI056277

PERIPHERAL VISION

First published in 2020 by
The Dedalus Press
13 Moyclare Road
Baldoyle
Dublin D13 K1C2
Ireland

www.**dedaluspress**.com

ISBN 978 1 910251 66 9 (paperback)

Dedalus Press titles are available in Ireland
from Argosy Books (www.argosybooks.ie) and in the UK
from Inpress Books (www.inpressbooks.co.uk).
Printed in Dublin by Digital Print Dynamic.

Cover design: Pat Boran

The Dedalus Press receives financial assistance from
The Arts Council / An Chomhairle Ealaíon.

PERIPHERAL VISION

PADDY BUSHE

DEDALUS PRESS

ACKNOWLEDGEMENTS

Primary acknowledgement must go to the artists, living and dead, well-known or anonymous, who created the sources. Is ar scáth a chéile a mhairimid. A special thank you is due to those creators whom I know personally, and who have enriched my own life, artistically and otherwise.

I wish to acknowledge a 2015 residency in Le Centre Culturel Irlandais in Paris, where this book was conceived and took its initial shape. The warm welcome and stimulation I was lucky enough to experience there was enormously encouraging. I also wish to acknowledge a 2018 Irish Writers' Centre residency in St. Mark's Church, Florence, where I was also warmly welcomed and encouraged. I am very grateful for both residencies, and I hope those who granted them are pleased with the results.

Some of these poems, or versions of them, were first published or broadcast in the following:

Cyphers, Herrings (The Aldeburgh Poetry Festival), *Irish Arts Review, Poetry Ireland Review, Southword, Sunday Miscellany* (RTÉ Radio 1), *The Irish Times, The Strokestown Anthology, The Temenos Academy Review* and *Reading the Future: New Writing from Ireland,* an anthology complied and edited by Alan Hayes to celebrate 250 years of Hodges Figgis.

Contents

~

⌒

AUTHOR'S NOTE

The poems in this collection arise from my engagement as a poet
with examples of various other artforms, from the prehistoric to the
contemporary. Hence the title *Peripheral Vision*. I use that title to
emphasise the peripherality of the poems to their sources; if they live
as poems, they may not even be aware of their ancestry. Many of the
sources are very well-known. Others are little-known, ephemeral and
perhaps not even works of art in the conventional sense. I engaged
with infinitely more works than I have written about, but the choice
of what to write about was not a matter of artistic evaluation. Many
of the works I contemplated moved me greatly but not into poetry.
The nature of the choice remains random, mysterious — essentially a
matter of a spark being ignited, or not.

I have written some very basic and fragmentary notes on the
sources at the end of this book. But, to echo the collection's title,
they are very peripheral to the poems. Interested readers may wish to
glance at some or all of them. They are not essential.

for Bernard O'Donoghue

I

A Vision of a Sunbeam Hung with Glasses

Right now, having for the umpteenth time
Mislaid all the glasses I have, even the pair strung
Around my neck, I remember the story of Brigid

And how she hung her dripping cloak miraculously
On a sunbeam that, shafting through her cell window,
Shone there steadfastly until the cloak was dry.

And so, looking out the window at a drizzly day —
Now even more smeared and blurred — I have
A vision: a sudden dazzlement of sunbeams

Erupting from behind the clouds, one of which —
One single lovely sunbeam — blazes an unerring path
Straight through my window, branching into slivers

So perfect for hanging glasses that you'd never miss them,
Each pair vying for attention, delightful in the floating dust.

An Abundance of Glasses

When I spilled them out on the table —
The dozen or so pairs of reading glasses
I'd got in the chain store for a throwaway
Couple of Euro a pair — I smiled and thought
I'd never again find myself searching
And muttering self-reproaches. Glinting
In cheerful yellow and pink packaging,
They winked reassurance, linked wide-open
Frames like a glittering music-hall chorus.

It was weeks afterwards that I dredged up
The image that had tugged like an undertow:
A smeared window, a cement floor, a broken
Sunbeam snagged on a heap of wire-framed
Glasses, almost all round-lensed, some broken,
Tangled like barbed wire, a *danse macabre*
Challenging onlookers to believe what they see,
Begging them never again to shut their eyes. A cello
Played in the yard outside, *adagio cantabile*.

Peripheral Vision

The way we see things is affected by what we know or what we believe.
— John Berger, *Ways of Seeing*

Given her age and where she came from, it was,
He thought, small wonder Colly started to see things
After the burial of her daughter. That was when

She forgot to ensure the dead woman's clothes
Were worn to Mass before any other wearing.
She knew she had, for good or evil, crossed a line.

Things. *Beings.* Clustered high up in corners
Where rafters had once absorbed shadows
From outside the pool of her lamplit childhood.

They were mostly kind, and meant her no harm,
She'd say. They usually came at the fall of night,
And were like a kind of company, you know,

For someone like herself who was now alone.
Moreover, they reminded her of the old days
And of the old people and the things they knew.

But sometimes, they frightened her, especially
The older one dressed in white, who combed her hair
And muttered from the ceiling, for hours on end.

She was a bad one, Colly knew, for all her *plámás*,
And they couldn't both stay in the one house.
She'd get agitated then, voice raised, eyes restless,

And once he visited to find her standing on a chair,
Flailing at the ceiling with her walking-stick,
Red and breathless with rage and imprecation.

Do you believe in the fairies, Colly? He coaxed
Her down, trying to gentle his way into her mind.
I don't believe in them, but I know they're there.

He climbed onto the chair and stretched his hand
Towards the high corner, stared into its dustiness.
There's nothing here, Colly, nothing at all to see.

Yes, but listen and I'll tell you something now,
 Colly confided, as he sat earnestly across from her,
That will explain all that once you think about it.

*The eye-doctor told me I had a kind of blindness
That means I see the sideways things differently.
You see, I see things that other people can't see.*

He recalled his own glaucoma, the medication
He dropped each day into both eyes, to deal,
The ophthalmologist said, with peripheral blindness.

Small wonder, he mused, making his way home,
That Colly sees the things she knows are there.

Restoration

for Tim Horgan

(i)

He had entered the painting before its restoration,
Had been drawn to its headland, been buffeted
By those onshore winds hammering angular waves
Into its steely sea, heard the cacophony of seabirds

Snatching at its surface. He had felt his whole being
Stretching to the horizon, felt the occluded sun's
Enormous lightness coaxing him up to its painted
Self, its universal eye. But he had stood forlornly

In the foreground, felt the grit of the blown sand
Sting his cheeks, had narrowed his clouding eyes
And mind towards dullness. The seabirds cried
In mourning down the cold wind as he retreated

Out of the painting that, layer upon layer, had become
A place he might have been. He ached for realisation.

(ii)

After the restoration, he walked back into the painting.
And couldn't believe his eyes. He heard the same cries
Of the seabirds, felt the same sand blown by the same
Boisterous wind flinging its ragged self at the headland.

But these now were votive cries, votive incense thrown
Indiscriminately in one great raucous blaring of *I am.*
Varnishings unpeeled themselves from his amazed eyes,
As he marvelled at this fanfare of the common world.

Here and now the sun had come into its own, its own
Give and take, take and give with the sea and the clouds
That nuanced themselves from the profoundest indigo
To purest azure dancing delighted steps across the sky.

And he too was revivified, became part of the restoration,
Freshly embodied in — say it, yes, he dared — a revelation.

II

Imogen's Wings

for Imogen Stuart

In the sunlit courtyard, the great stone curves
Of those wings you sculpted take on the shine
And depth of the fresh chestnuts sprinkled

All over the grass and gravelled paths below,
And engrave the frosty air like cello-music,
A valediction forbidding mourning of the seasons.

Monumentally still, they flit constantly
Between one shape and the same other,
One for sorrow, two for joy. The space between

Those feathered slabs could encompass a globe,
Or a fallen chestnut. Their uplifted tips
Aspire like the peaks of Skellig Michael.

That white dove that flew into the Latin
Of Columbanus nestles here, gurgling warm
Approval of all this international to and fro,

Cradling it within its soft, bulging spaces.
But here too is the rush of sterner wings,
That surge of anger when you beat the air

With powerful words and swooped on those
Who dared profane that wing-haunted island.
Here are the militant wings of the Archangel.

Imogen, imagine if you will your powerful wings
Enfolding, embracing Skellig. Now the stone sings.

Centre Culturel Irlandais, Paris, October 2015

21

A Moonlight Waltz

From a great distance a poet has heard
The sad strains of its gaiety, and knows

That, like so many others, it will end
In a tristesse the creative heart knows well.

On the beach, under the moon, the dancers
Sense nothing of this. They know only

The whirl, the glide, the hum of spheres
Delighting in their every step and turn

And turnabout, rapt in an exhilaration
Of shining eyes and silver laughter, gilded

Arms and shoulders catching the light.
The musicians are shadowed by the cliff,

Apart from one whose lifted face slants
Into light, his ear cocked for every nuance,

His fingers on the fretted lute patterning
Every last thing he hears and sees.

Do not be fooled by the gaudy clothes,
The amused eyes, the knowing smile.

This one hears the echo of what is to come.
He knows the score. He'll soon strike a chord.

Scallop

These fluted curves encompass every sound
The world makes, hinged between sea and sky.
They hear those voices that will not be drowned.

Pilgrims once gathered here, praying aloud,
Holding their shells aloft to feel the bright
And radiant curves encompass every sound.

Love, too, drifted lightly ashore, and wound
Her salt-blown hair through earthly songs to tie
Herself to voices that will not be drowned.

And the lone voyagers — poor souls who found
Nor god nor love — they too sit high and dry
Where fluted shells encompass every sound.

Shingle whispers constantly, shifting its ground
To help the village brace against the tide,
Determined that its voices will not drown.

These are human shades that crowd around
Where tides ebb and flow, gods live and die.
These fluted curves encompass every sound
And hear those voices that will not be drowned.

Shaping Spirit

for Catriona O'Connor

See water at the far

      End of time wearing

Stone away with grain

      Upon grain of sand

Thrown by wave

      After wave's explosion

And yet stone never

      Wearing away

Water that shifts

      Wave after wave

Into the shape

      Of water-shaped stone

The Artist Among the Mountains

Although he had brought his pencils,
Charcoal and pastels in his rucksack

Along with his folding canvas stool
That day he trekked into the high

Mountain valley, he never felt the need
To use his sketchbook. He just unfolded

The stool, spread the tripod legs
Evenly, wedging them between clefts

Of rock and clumps of knotty heather,
And sat there the whole day. He watched

The peaks above the snowline circling him
With the curiosity of a herd, saw them

Lose their fear and settle again to ruminate.
He saw how the clouds became the snow

Around the peaks, how snow and clouds
Picked out each summit's ultimate shape,

Folding and unfolding it with infinitely
Patient attention to every changing detail.

His breathing slowed, deepened. He felt
Himself expand, felt his shoulders flex

Themselves skyward, knew the muscularity
Of rocks and ledges along his bones, the flow

Of meltwater through his veins. He realised
He was being drawn into the mountains,

Knew he was his own parchment, on which
The mountains were working. He braced

His boots like fenceposts in the rough ground
That he might let his mind climb into clouds.

Much later, descending towards the village,
He knew the mountains were already painted.

Thumb

for Maura Dooley

(i)

The dedication? The truth is I mixed up sculptors
At the Pompidou Centre, where a ten-metre

Golden thumb dominated the square outside,
Backgrounded by a hoarding for a Jim Dine exhibition,

And I assumed *Thumb* was his and then I thought
Of your 'Cleaning Jim Dine's Heart', and I thought

Of a possible companion piece, so here I am —
Serendipitously mistaken — offering this poem to you.

(ii)

Here, then: César's *Thumb*. He must have smiled
At that echo of absolute power of life and death.

Yet so much life rests in this raised insouciance
That, like your *Heart*, has everything in it. So like

All other thumbs and yet so much itself, its whorled
Thumbprint a singular universal, an irreproducible

Intricacy that repeats *we are* as it repeats *I am*,
Holding itself stubbornly up against all good reason.

This *Thumb*, like *Heart*, has room for everything.
Sucking wisdom into itself, it becomes oracular,

Inclining its cowled head towards passers by,
A thumbnail like the pattern of all countenance,

A head bowed now and again in acquiescence,
Above all, bowed in constant acknowledgement.

Piper

for Bob Ó Cathail

Quietly, then, the piper begins. Settled in his chair,
He elbows the bellows, coaxing long sighs
While searching for tunings in resonant air.

He pipes up a rooster who raucously declares
Daybreak at midnight with all its hues and cries,
But doesn't stir himself, rests easy in the chair.

He pipes up a fox-chase, pipes the running hare
And pipes the thrush who pipes the reasons why
Love's grace-notes travel wide, glittering in the air.

Now he pipes the howl of women in despair
Where torn, bloody flags and broken bodies lie.
The piper makes no move, rooted in the chair.

A nimbus of afterlight settles like a prayer
As old notes linger when a tune has gone by
And passed upward into high, remote air.

His head's thrown back. Light ripples through his hair.
The earth exhales in drones, the chanter scales the sky.
Although the piper barely stirs, rooted in the chair,
He travels deep and wide, layering tremulous air.

The Piper's Exhalation

for Carlos Núñez

Because his whole heart
And soul overflowed

With the air that inspired him,
And because his *gaita* likewise

Had inhaled almost to bursting
The music of what happens,

The piper snatched a moment
From his throbbing mouthpiece

To exhale into the gobsmacked air
An ululation resounding somewhere

Between a howl and a whoop
Of exultation over Galicia.

The Raven's Lamentation

His croaking aches for *portaireacht,* for the bubbling
Of shorebirds, for the dance tunes of thrush and ouzel

Invisibly silvering the air from among the branches,
For larksong losing the run of itself in tumbling skies.

The raven notes all this, craves all this, but knows
It will not be his. He grieves that only the drones

Answer him, grieves that no piped note will ever jig
Or reel him to enchantment. Only villages mourning

Their battle-dead, only a howling against famine
Or against the old malice of the sea will summon

The harsh inevitability of his music. Over and over
He mourns his solitary way down the stony wind.

The Hour of the Day

He feels the floor tilt, tipping him towards
A different plane as soon as he draws

The bow smoothly across incredulous strings
That are beside themselves with excitement.

Even his feet lose the run of themselves, slide
Down from under him. No matter, he is pure

Spirit, his music drawing him up and out
Of himself, of the room and into the clouds,

Where he stays for the length of a few tunes,
As he does, at this hour, every morning.

Workshop

So this is where the whole things starts:
With rasp, vice, anvil, pincers, chisel,
All these instruments for soaring. Here

Is what polishes marble to smooth passage
Across immeasurable skies, burnishes vast
Distances in brass, measures the depth

Of a kiss in stone, of an infant's dreams.
Here is celestial toil: bird, pillar and orb,
To be hammered and tonged, hoisted

And pulleyed up and over themselves
Into space, into shapes beyond weight,
Beyond recognition, discovering shapes

Beyond instruments. And to return to be
Worked on again. The whole thing again.

The Art of Belief

But sometimes the artist will lead you
And your amazed eyes where reason

Absolutely refuses to go. A painted saint, say,
His long, bony fingers — a piper's, maybe —

Joined so delicately just at their very tips,
Arched and opened around a universe,

Are buttressing what you will not believe,
Making vaulted certainty of the air between,

As if a great bronze door has been opened
To reveal the very entrails of conviction.

And the air, being spun of filigreed gold
All around him, sings notes you know

You cannot hear. But still you see them
Embodied here, tangible beyond belief.

The Gilt Seahorses of Nossa Senhora del Rosario

for Melissa Newman

The altar bulged with baroque *buaileam sciath,*
Resplendent with rococo razzmatazz,
Glorious with the gilt of its grandeur!
Here was *mór is fiú* and braggadocio,
Here the weighty worthiness of a world
Dazzled by itself! And dazed. And drained.
Casting his eyes to the ground, Jesus wept.

Until from under bent brows, to left and right,
Halfway up each ponderous framing column,
He made out two curling seahorses,
Who each flicked a gilt, translucent tail,
Rested its long equine jaw on a ledge
And sent him messages in speech bubbles.
Lifting his eyes to heaven, Jesus winked.

Chrysalis Smiles

for Darragh Morgan and Siripong Albert Tiptan

And it was just then, just at the very moment
The music had climbed almost to overreaching,

But had steadied in time into perfect pitch
Like a roped climber upright on a sharp ridge,

That the two violinists smiled at one another
Momentarily across continents. Their smiles,

Wriggling themselves up and out through arched
And concentrated brows, thrummed and spiralled

Upwards like a pair of butterflies in a Chinese story
To settle in chandeliered splendour overhead.

From where they beamed down on the quintet,
On the amazed violas daring themselves to follow,

On the cello sawing through its melancholy depths,
On the piano, lightening itself, preparing for flight.

Raising the Siege

Wearily I raise my staff, invoking ancient arts
Against the wolves who howl outside the walls
Through this long, brutal siege of the heart.

Iron bands squeeze tighter, the city starves.
The air is frozen with omens of downfall.
Fearful, I clutch my staff, uncertain of my art.

We walk the city, a place now utterly apart.
Windows reflect only ourselves, appalled
At this implacable siege of the heart.

Shadows outside swell, begin to be heard
As chain-linked rhythm, as sinister footfall
Growing loud, denouncing the staff of art.

The spirit freezes. Our own souls grow hard.
The inevitable claws at us, as time crawls
Along besieged passageways of the heart.

And still we cry out for a blaze against the dark
In full knowledge of the final, ineluctable fall.
Resolved, I lift our staff, invoking all my art
To raise once more the endless siege of the heart.

A Poet in Bronze

He's statued outside the house
Where he was born and grew up
Spellbound by nearby church bells.

But the poet's face, like all the faces
He ever had, or pretended to have,
Is hidden by a huge, bronze book

Bearing just two words, engraved
One to the front, one to the back:
The city's name, the poet's name.

I laugh, reminded again of my father
Remonstrating with me: *why must
Your nose be forever stuck in a book?*

The Poem Rescued

I

The clergy wanted to own the poem:
The where and when, the how
And why of it. The whole of it.

They insisted its provenance must
Be ordained, its utterance mediated
And sanctioned by the initiated.

They didn't want the sunlight
To gild it, nor to find its shadows;
Didn't want it to hear the traffic.

They didn't want any passers-by
To stare, thinking they recognised
A neighbour, or a long-lost friend.

They were adamant the poem
Needed shelter, needed above all
Not to have notions about itself.

So they raised it high into a niche
Among the other statued poems
That lined the cathedral's walls.

The poem's slow tears welled
Into stone, calcified into a narrative
Priests would decode for pilgrims.

II

Unauthorised, but with a forged
Name-card hanging around its neck,
A song slipped in with the pilgrims,

And went down secretly to the crypt,
Where it disembodied itself
Into invisibility, and hid the name-card.

Quietly the song began to hum itself
Under its breath, for the time being
Audible only to the surrounding dead.

Then, still all the while invisible,
It made its way back up to the nave
Step by step beginning to be heard,

Amplifying its multiple voices
Until it filled the great cathedral
Silencing the voices of the priests.

Magnifying itself along the soaring
Stained glass windows, it scaled
Pillars and vaulting arches, and pulled

Itself into the huge bronze cupola,
A breathing space for its dizzy self
And for the tiny searching faces,

Awestruck and infinitely far below.
They heard it resonate in the dome,
Heard it surpass its words and music,

Heard it become planetary ripples,
Infinite. Unseen, the song descended
And, taking the poem by the hand,

Walked unhindered down the aisle,
Unlocked the bronze doors and led
The way out into the sunlit square.

Here they strolled, found a café, dallied
Over coffee on the terrace, smiling
At passers-by who sometimes smiled back.

III

Statuesque

for Laurence Edwards

The man bends under the weight of the cuttings
He will draw home. He has spent the day hewing
The small branches and shoots permitted him.

The leaves and twigs will feed the cow. She is tethered
Because he owns no grazing. The branches will keep
The fire smouldering. We will manage, he thinks.

His load is tied with pieces of thin rope,
Tightened beyond all measure. The pack grows
Dense, its branches scored by the rope's pressure.

When he heaves it onto his shoulders, sinews
And branches knot into each other, the man grows
Into his load, his load an impetus to raise him up

In silhouette against the light. You might imagine him
Heroic, bronzed. Imagine something noble in all this.

The Sleep of Reason Creates Monsters

Prophecy's black candles cast a deep shadow.
Monsters are rumoured, name by whispered name.
Reason has slept and is waking to madness.

Succession now falls on the fool and the gambler,
Jokers and knaves have trumped the royal game.
Prophecy's black candles cast a deep shadow.

The play's at the bidding of bankers and barons
Whose winnings are counted below the dark flames.
Reason has slept and is waking to madness.

If drilling or poison make the rich land barren
The people are schooled and will know who to blame.
The ones who are Other inhabit deep shadows.

Those who dissent should know what will happen:
The managed confessions in the public squares
Where Reason still sleeps, but will waken to madness.

If the tower cannot reap, the tower then will harrow.
In the cellars are ledgers and instruments of shame.
Prophecy's black candles have cast a deep shadow
Where Reason once slept. We have woken to madness.

Wednesday, November 9th, 2016

During Donald Trump's Inauguration

I closed my eyes, to conjure from the 1950s
An image of that towering man Paul Robeson
Singing his heart and soul across the border

Between Washington State and Canada,
When tides of race and power and wealth
Surged all as one to try to drown him out,

Snatching his passport lest his songs be heard
By the Mine, Mill and Smelter Workers Union.
I conjured the noisy flatback truck manoeuvred

To the border, and the straining loudspeakers
Bearing the burden of his songs where his masters
Feared to grant him passage. And I conjured

All those gathered thousands rising to *Joe Hill*,
To *Ol' Man River* and to *Let My People Go,* rising
To anthems that might crack dividing walls.

And this still I hoard: that profound voice rolling
Across the barriers built by poisoned money,
Urgent with the wish to make America good.

In a Walled Garden

There are street noises. Church bells overhead
Reassure me. Things being normal as they seem,
I cannot believe what is now being said.

Officials have warned against being misled
Into outdated loyalties, to beware of extreme
Threats in our streets to the church bells overhead.

People have disappeared. Officials say they've fled —
Clear evidence of a plot against the regime.
It's hard to believe what I sometimes hear said.

At night, sirens. They fill the air with dread,
Then urgent steps, warnings. Sometimes a scream
Muffled by street noise, church bells overhead.

Outside my wall's barred window, sullen as lead,
The river crawls by, inexorably. Downstream,
The sewers overflow with what's being said.

But here there is calm, order. A wall, a hedge,
Shelter me. In the sunlight, I can sit and dream
Of ordinary street noise, church bells overhead.
I must not begin to believe what's being said.

Dance of the City

On walls, under arches, the whole city chants
An anthem that swells and sways through the crowd.
Here are many as one in one swirling dance.

The winter's been long. The palace remains harsh.
But the dance in the streets has emptied each house
And on walls, under arches, the whole city chants.

By churches and markets the dancers advance
And retreat, high-steppingly proud
Of being many as one in one swirling dance.

The pulse of the dancing is lifting those hearts
That were wounded, those heads that were bowed.
On walls, under arches, the whole city chants

Then one who is breathless is all at once grasped
And linked and uplifted, spun and spun around
By the song of the many into one swirling dance.

The courtiers in the palace are watching aghast,
Watching the dancers, hearing songs sung out loud
On walls, under arches. The whole city chants
Of the many as one in this one swirling dance.

Badhbh

The raven and the carrion crow raise hooded heads,
Beaks bloodied from the tearing, to croak gratitude,

Salutations to their goddess sister, who has once more
Scattered rich pickings. The spread of severed limbs,

They know, is an earnest of so much more to come.
She gallops high above the carnage, her black horse

Fragmenting the sky, her cry a triumphant howling
Of sirens. She always carries the day, no matter

Who claims victory, or the right to victory. Today
The city's theatres and cafés bleed. Tomorrow

Frontier villages will crumple, will be hung with votive
Images of the city's dead. She will ride a white horse.

Light

(i)

A single light serves many purposes. The same
Lantern that clarifies the confusion in the square,

And allows the execution squads to do their work,
Shines too on the final defiance of the partisans,

Allows their people to remember how they died,
Eyes gleaming, fists raised, allows their last words

To hang as an illuminated banner in the anthemic air,
A banner to light the many dark gatherings to come.

(ii)

There is too the light gleaming from attics and cellars
Where gatherings whisper accounts of the newly dead

And, under bare bulbs that light dusty corners, create
A manifesto to spread its light in circles that widen

To encompass the earth. This is the light that will guide
The men at screens who will guide the men with bombs,

And the screens themselves will light in silent celebration
Of attics and cellars darkened, of screams never heard.

(iii)

This is not to say that the execution squads see light
In the way the partisan sees it, nor that the torturer

Knows light with the same clarity as his spotlit victim.
This is not to say the king believes in the burning cross

He ignites for his people to flock towards, nor is this
To deny those heroes who, dazzled, die by the light.

It is just to plead for a light less endless, less relentless.
It is to say that pure light burns eyes from their sockets.

Piobrachd

for David Power

Dark women wail in the midst of the slaughter,
As though the earth itself exhaled suffering, sounds
Never before known, never to be known hereafter.

Here's feral lamentation. Drones howl down chanter
Until the ground plays itself like an open wound
And dark women wail in the midst of the slaughter.

They have heard old keenings, fragments of folklore
Preserved by elders, but have never before howled
Such a savage harrowing. Nor will they do hereafter.

The rites will come later, the sprinkling of water.
There will be processions and the raising of mounds.
Now dark women wail in the midst of the slaughter.

Here are the fields and the ruins they fought for,
The meeting hall, the place of worship. They vow,
Having wailed so fiercely, never to wail hereafter.

And still there are anthems. Still sons and daughters
Sing words of old anthems not yet drowned out
By dark women wailing in the midst of the slaughter.
Still the anthems are taught. And will be sung hereafter.

The White Bear

The great rolling hindquarters are urgent
With momentum. He is charged with the need
To make good the season, to hunt in lucent
Monochromes of sky and ice and water,
To bloody the lunging paws, and then to sleep
In darkness comforted by memories of light.

But he hesitates, reluctant forepaws digging in
Against the unexpected tilt of the floe.
His raised head moves slowly, like a scanner.
He hears the bellowing of many glaciers
Calving out of their time, gets a warm smell
He doesn't yet know. Knows it must be feared.

War Pipes

A piper long astray
In the Cave of Gold
And in his wits
For generations
Past and to come
Playing night and day
Maddened into prayer
For one thing only
A third hand he craved
That might grasp a sword.

IV

Family Meal

Again, the same dream. He's outside
The window of his own house.
Again he has locked himself out.

There is a table, pooled in light.
There is a family, an evening meal.
There is a woman, a boy, a girl

Facing the silhouette of a man
Whose unlit back is to the window.
The girl stares towards both men,

Sees only the man in the room. The man
Outside does not recognise the dark
Bulk of the man the girl watches

In the lamplight. Nor can he hear
Anything she says across the table
Or any answer the man may make.

The rigid smile she hides behind
Shows nothing of the icy shards
He feels encircle her heart and eyes.

He knows it well now, this dream
Where he has locked himself outside.
Years and years too late he beats

At window glass that will not shatter
But echoes dully like hammered
Lead weights around his guilty heart.

A Postcard from Knossos

for Pat Boran

Dedalus, on the other hand, always knew
Exactly what he was doing, being wary
Of high flyers, of the big splash, of playing
To the gods. He liked to push simple things —
A cow-hide, feathers, wax, a ball of string —
Right to their limits in great undertakings,
In labyrinths of death, in tracing the intricacies
Of love's secret passages, but not beyond.

Here, where it all started, he's known still
As a down-to-earth man. Extraordinarily so.

Faustina Shivers

She knows no shame for that
Formed part of the bargain
When she sold her soul
Just a normal transaction
It cannot be called diabolical
She tells her everyday self
A corporate takeover of a soul
Regularly she checks the locks
On visions outside of contract
And wanders abandoned rooms
A shiver in endless search
Of a backbone to land on

Triptych for a Neighbour

in memoriam Eddie Falvey

(i) EARLY POTATOES

This spring, again, I remember how every year,
The first fine February day that came, he'd say
It's a bit soon, but God knows maybe I might
Throw down a *dorn* of earlies in the morning.

To imagine a gauntlet being thrown down
Is fanciful, I know. But as I sort this year's
Sprouted seed, he's again over my shoulder,
And he's once more shaking his fist at winter.

(ii) LANDING

I remember too the day he swore his wits
Were gone astray, with the fright he'd got
From my garden Buddha he'd seen silhouetted
On the cliff, meditating on the conjunction
Of sea and land and sky. He had glanced up
Just as he landed, right on a top-tide swell,
After a spin out with the lads. Never before,
He said, did it loom over him quite like that.

I seldom go to sea myself now, just an odd spin
In the kayak around Carraig Éanna and its seals,
Avoiding the reefs he'd shown me. Hauling pots
In a hard wind is just a memory. But I still know
To keep my bow into the swell, to watch for
The backwash off the rock, for a north-westerly
Rising on hot afternoons. Above all, he warns,
You must keep your wits about you on the sea.

(iii) EARLY MAY GALE

Today, the fifteenth of the month, the early May
Gale he foresaw every year is blowing itself out,
Shaking the white blossoms just starting to come
On what promises to be a good crop of earlies,

If, as it should, the gale settles with the sea. Buddha,
I am sure, senses the lovely foliage over his shoulder,
But contemplates only the sea, as if to keep all our keels
Even, our wits about us, on sea, on land, in all seasons.

The Bell for Order

i.m. Eamon Langford

You always sang that the October *wind*
(to rhyme with *kind)* sang around
The Castle of Dromore. It suited you,
The old-fashioned correctness, the urge

To do the right thing. And so you did
In the Corner House, tinkling the little bell
For good order for all the performers,
Each one in their own time and space.

Such a sweet passing bell! The sea-swell
That seized your heart next day in Kells
Was just a ripple, a tinkle, but enough
To call for order, gently. It suited you.

Now there's the ordinary sound of wind
Around Iveragh, lamenting one of a kind.

Candle

Afterwards he
Circled his arms
Around her
Joined his hands
As if in prayer
Bowed his head
To the incense
Of her
Spread hair
Flickered
Asleep awake
Intense
Alpha
Incandescent
Omega
A candle
Awaiting everyday
Resurrection
Ascending
Into flame.

The Configuration of Love

We made love the night you turned sixty-nine.
No, not that playful configuration of the young,

But configured still, and still configuring
Trajectories that veer now and again

Towards infinity, on axes of time, of space.
And as we drift, elliptically into sleep

Trajectories dissolve, axes dissolve,
Become random, serendipitous. Like stars.

Afternoon in Olhao

When, after love, the celebratory sun
Slants through the shutters on me

Clinging into your curved back
With my face in your tousled hair,

I nuzzle into the memory of half
A century ago, your uniformed

Back curved into me as I crossbar
You back to school, daring to lean

Into the curve, daring to inhale
Such lifetimes, such fragrances!

A Bracelet from Florence

Crossing the *Ponte Vecchio* that spans
The narrowest point of the Arno below,
I brooded again on that capricious throw
Of the dice that upended all our plans
For you to join me here. One untied lace
Was all it took, one awful breathless fall
To clarify our fragility, and clarify all
That sunders us, and sunders place from place.

Enough of that. A nameless bridge in Cork
Being where you broke your wrist, I thought
Of *caol*, of span, of the hurt hand I long
To kiss. So in a jewellery shop I picked
A token of so much we both have missed,
And bring this silver bracelet for your wrist.

> *"caol" in Irish means both "wrist" and "narrow",*
> *sometimes specifically the narrow part of a river.*

V

Afternoon Pilgrimage

for Antonio Raúl de Toro Santos

Because it had been said we must visit
Santo André de Teixido while we live,
Or else be spirited there later as toads

Or lizards, we set off down the steep path
Marked by votive cairns and stitched tightly
Into tumbled granite by sea-pink and crocus,

Clambering down ladders of heat and light
And along a path beaten through yew trees
Whose shadowing gave the village its name.

Mica and quartzite flashed here and there
Among the boulders, whispering insistently
About that otherworld long since denied.

The path steadily dipped and dropped
Along abrupt zigzags that turned back
On themselves like an endless argument,

Down to orange tiles, stone walls and narrow
Twisting lanes pungent with dung and straw,
Then the village, the fountain, the church

Pied with slated stone and gleaming mortar,
Overflowing with candlelight and painted
Breadcrumb statues hawked in the square.

And as we left, past the parking area jammed
With buses, and along the double yellow lines
Of the new access road, it was hard to make out

Which way we had come down, which world
We had entered or left or which way back up
Would lead to wherever it was we'd been going.

In a Hammock in Galicia

for José Miguel Giraldez

Moulded into a net hammock
      Moored between two trees
In an orchard sloping south,

      The light through a mesh of leaves
Stippling dewdropped windfalls.
      And somewhere, children playing,

I think of the Milesians
      Who, they say, left these parts
To settle on Ireland's west coast,

      And of Amergin, who claimed
He was wind and wave and weather,
      Sun and moon and stars.

I laugh, not quite out loud.
      The hammock sways, just a little.
Nearby, a peach drops into silence.

The Place of Prayer

The afternoon light in this place of prayer
Is luminous with honey and amber. The place

Could be outdoors, a forest of birch, say,
In late October. Or it could be sunlight

Shafting through stained glass, pinpointing
Dust motes pendant in air that's tremulous

With long waiting for something to happen,
Or mourning something which already has.

There is, insistent but still in the background,
The heavy rhythm of slow, painstaking trains.

Here the visible shrinks, becomes the audible,
Becomes the utterance of the unsayable.

Light and texture, even the faint smell of ashes,
Are a susurration of words woven into prayer,

The warp and weft of which now rise and fall
Into patterns that are pure sound, moanings

Of disbelief that repeat themselves over
And over until they whisper, barely, *we believe*.

Amergin's Ship

for Holger Lönze

Because he wanted simply to be as one
With the swelling wave and the wind,

With the salmon and with the stars
Clustered in the eye of the gannet,

He sailed north when the four winds
Blossomed together in a compass,

North being the petal that trembled
Towards the grey ambiguous headlands

The elder swore he scried from the tower
Infinitely far beyond the salty horizon.

The ship's skin-lined planking breathed
Brine and wind, welded gust and swell

In a coupling that surpassed navigation.
Sea and ship hammered one another

Into one another's shape, shaped
Wind and weather to the poet's will

To be the voyage, to be the landfall
And the words that marked the landfall,

To be the land and the land's creatures
To be the stones raised in commemoration,

To be the ship beached forever on the land,
And the words singing themselves into bronze.

Shaping the Place of Speech

for John Carey

Absorbing soft vowels
From the formless air

      From the exhalations
      Of river, lake and sea;

Enclosed by the consonants
Of summits, shores and ridges

      That stretch towards horizons
      Veering between planes;

Punctuated by raised stones
That yearn for articulacy,

      Yearn to be monuments
      Set far down and firm;

Conjured again and again
By the poet's incantations,

      The place becomes landscape
      Shaped to its own utterance.

Dance

for Karen Hendy

At first your dance steps are slow.
Slow. Slow as the black bog's
Ooze and seep swallowing
Leaf and branch, root and bole,
Whispering ineluctable decay.

A bubbling, then, in the dark.
Tentative. And slow. Tentative,
Tentative, tentative and then pat
-terns appear and disappear and
Then tapping and tapping and tap.

And the oakwood echoing, echoing
To the patterned blows of axe upon
Axe for charcoal, for smelting, for iron
In the soul, and blitzkrieg advance and
Advance and advance on the land.

Retreat now, into the blackbird's sweet
Song on the blossoming briar. Ease
Your heart into airiness, your steps
Into stars patterning the sky, hands
Bridging all gaps. All abask. All aglow.

The Dispute about the Immaculate Conception

The woman around whom the dispute
Is centred, is herself outside the circle,

As of now above it. She throws her eyes
To Heaven. Whether her eyes,

Her outstretched arms casting aside
The dark cloak from her scarlet robe

Are submissive or despairing or just
Exasperated, she is not in a position

To tell us. All the words are below,
Being rolled out on scrolls by cherubs

Or pointed at by distinguished men,
Their mitres and books held by boys

Who are bored now but will learn.
Just one young scholar is doubtful,

Raises a questioning eye towards her.
But he does not disturb the dispute

Which circles around words, such as
Concupiscence, virginity, conception.

Below the circle of disputation, two
Naked lovers lie sleeping, satisfied.

When the circle turns, as it now
And again will do, they will be above.

Pietà

Christ lay stretched, broken yet heroic
In his mother's arms, she exaltedly
In mourning, her soul now magnified

As she held that embodied sacrifice
Close to her, laying it open also
To receive the world's homage.

The broken body of a man, the robed
Woman in mourning. The old pattern
Becoming a pattern for a new order.

Jesus retched. Wounded Jesus refused
That which had been ordained, refused
The burial, the tomb, the heroic repetition.

Reaching up, he wiped his mother's face
Clear of its exaltation, its magnificent grief,
Of all but the comfort and grief that must be.

Androgynously, then, he arose and cradled her,
Became his mother comforting her infant self,
Refusing that which was eternally ordained.

And this was the true, and will be the everlasting
Resurrection of Christ, the consolation of his mother.

The Road to God Knows Where

for Seán Hardie

Especially when a milky sky and a pale
Dusty road that had ranged the valley
Has dissolved itself in that white opacity;

Especially when this gleaming fluency
Separates itself, and a rolling fog sours
What is left of the day; then the long road

To God knows where snakes back on itself,
Sloughing off all knowledge, and all at once
Nowhere is there any road, and God is nowhere.

Listener

If you would listen well, and truly hear
Rumours from below the clay, leave space
Between the cupped hand and the waiting ear,

And listen to the deep earth. All of the dear
Dead are still singing, or whispering prayers
That you may listen, and may truly hear.

Grant all of them entrance, grant them clear
Passage in their own time, at their own pace,
Between the cupped hand and the listening ear.

Let long lost rivers break the surface here
Funnelling themselves into a sunlit race
That you can listen to, and truly hear.

Let children play here, play without fear
And jubilantly make it their own place
Between the cupped hand and the listening ear.

The faintest, furthest sound will be as near
As starlight silvering your upturned face
If you have listened well, and cherish what you hear
Between the cupped hand and the enlightened ear.

Solstice

Dubhluachair. Thin rush-light just
Enough to huddle around a word
That bears such a weight of darkness.

Black rushes. Dark light of the year
Whose turning is fearfully hoped for.
The dark of this stone row marks

The sun's deepest down descent
Behind the mountain horizon distant
Beyond any measure that we know,

Who know only to gather around hope
And hold close our circled rush-lights
Finding little spurts of warmth in words.

Íochtar Cua, 21 December 2017

Midwinter Sunset, Cill Rialaig

for Tomás Ó Carragáin

Outside, all day, a low
Dull begrudging light.
In the abbot's cell, our own dark
Cradles us, cradles
Our fearful selves locked
Together for the year's dying, praying
For fusion, for rebirth,
Willing our selves into one,
Into oneness with the One's earth.

Now the old light falters through
This slabbed passageway
Whose orientation we calculated
Into our sacred masonry.
We have built a tenebrous shelter
Of stones that are the bones of light.
We have listened to the stone. Now see
The light assert its way along the slabs,
Refracted once more to its true course.

Casting

Here, then, is beginning. Cowhide bellows
Settle into themselves, into rhythm.
Their rasping is the earth whispering

Its own deepest secrets to the furnace
Scooped into the ground, the caked walls
Shaped with fireclay, bound with dung.

Smoke- blackened faces now and again
Catch firelight, anxious eyes reflecting
A covenant against encroaching darkness.

A murmuring, a sudden urgent movement
Scatters a constellation of sparks.
The charcoal glows almost unbearably

And the crucible changes colour, throbs
Like a sea buffeted by a thunderstorm.
Someone tongs the crucible, holds it

A sacred moment, then pours a practised
Stream of molten ore to fill the mould.
There is a low ripple of approval, of relief.

Here, now, are bells to initiate ceremonies
And sound belief. Here are metal harpstrings
Drawn meticulously towards a fine sweetness.

And, raising its great curved head like a swan,
A bronze trumpet exhales the song of the earth
Proclaiming the moment of its eternal beginning.

Sky Woman

for Aya Takagi

She walks the sky, and combs the clouds for stars
Where there are none, because she's always yearned
For things that lie behind the things that are.

She loves to feel the earth, to walk the paths
Her people walk. But she was also born
To walk the sky and comb the clouds for stars.

A harebell's chime, a rowan's sudden flare,
She reads as signals that it's time to turn
Towards paths that lie beneath the paths that are.

The villagers have mapped the paths that mark
The routes for trade. Now only she discerns
The skyward paths that comb the clouds for stars.

She knows by heart the heavy laws they've carved
Deep into stone slabs. But she has also learned
The law that came before the laws that are.

And secretly she hoards an ancient shard
Of law inscribed upon a shattered urn:
Go walk the sky, go comb the clouds for stars,
And seek what lies beyond the things that are.

Woman, Moon and Mountain

for Lisbeth Mulcahy

There is a moon
Edged clean with frost
Rising in an indigo sky.

There is a mountain
Deep and dark-shadowed
Below silvered layers.

There is a woman
Crimson with the burden
Of the world's blood.

The woman, with all the strength
Of her outstretched limbs, yearns
For the moon and for the illumination
Of the moon's embrace. She howls,

Wordlessly, as once more the moon
Rises in heedless, bloodless splendour.
She retreats, once more, to the shelter
She has fashioned from the darkness.

The Piper Abroad

In the end he wanted to go home
To the island where salt winds,

In from the great ocean, droned
The winter long, until returning

Seabirds chanted exuberantly
Of migration as they nested.

He wanted it all, wanted the whole
Being there and not being there,

The leaving and the coming back,
Language and the loss of language,

The forgotten songs and their safe
Refuge in collectors' manuscripts.

He yearned for the island's cradle,
Yearned for its grave. And, yearning,

He played the lovely, fragmented
Uncertainties of the migrant heart.

Forging Icarus

... it was not an important failure. — W.H. Auden

In the end, then, is this — whatever importance
Or lack of it is attached — a simple failure?

To have gone towards and undergone
Such downright euphoria that height

And sea and sun were all the one
Wonderful tempering, to have been

Forged and fragmented and beaten
Whole in such fusion and fission

Of light that every last scrap of him
Was hammered into that great disc,

Still to reverberate day after perfect
Brazen day: is this no more than failure,

Important or otherwise? Now and again
The ploughman raises unhappy eyes

From his furrow, the shipping merchant
From his accounts, and they yearn.

First Day in Varnam

for Beena K.J.

And yes, believe it or not, below the veranda
Where our clothes, rinsed of travel dust,

Hang gratefully in the sunlight, there really is
Shaded by a great fig tree, a lotus pond

With frogs pulsing out something important
I do not understand. And I understood

Only here and there the wisdom a *bean feasa*
This morning rooted and plucked from the air

And clay and leaves. So much I do not grasp
Either here or there. But I have begun to see,

Opaquely, that here is something divinely
Of the earth, something earthily of the divine.

bean feasa: Gaelic for a wise woman with knowledge of herbal cures

Turning the Tune

for Steve Cooney

Sweet antipodean, you turn the globe of music
Upside down, sprinkling abundant grace notes
As your fresh footprints trace old songlines.

When you close those absorbent eyes, your guitar
Tightens itself into the strings of a blind harper
Whose music offers its hand across centuries.

Da mihi manum. Give me your hand. And now
Hemispheres spin into the mirrors of themselves,
Their tunes and turnings handed on, handed down

The long meridians of memory, across the latitudes
Of kinship. Here is where we choose our equator,
And align the axis on which our world will spin.

Tabhair dom do lámh. Here's a universe of hands
Turning tunes. *Uni versus.* Towards the one turning.

NOTES
(with reservations)

These notes about specific sources for the poems are offered as background material that may be of interest to some readers. I include them with some reservations, not least a hesitation to impose them on those sources. The poems are not intended to be *about* the various sources that partly gave rise to them. Indeed, in many cases they deal with concerns and insights that are very different from those of the sources. I intend the poems to stand or fall on their own. If they do not work independently of their sources, they cannot be seen to succeed as poems. I will be quite happy for readers not to consult these notes.

I

Peripheral Vision My own thoughts about how we experience and appropriate artistic work, as well as various personal experiences, were brought into focus when reading John Berger's book, a sentence from which is quoted as an epigraph.

A Vision of a Sunbeam Hung with Glasses The story of Brigid's cloak hanging miraculously on a sunbeam is found in the 7th century *Life of Saint Brigid* by Cogitosus.

An Abundance of Glasses The image referred to is a photograph by the Polish photographer Stanislaw Mucha taken after the Auschwitz-Birkenau concentration camp was liberated.

Restoration The painting referred to is *The Monk by the Sea* by Caspar David Friedrich, which was restored in 2015 (Alte Nationalgalerie, Berlin). The immediate context of the poem was my having cataracts removed.

II

Imogen's Wings Refers to Imogen Stuart's sculpture *The Flame of Human Dignity*, in the courtyard of the Centre Culturel Irlandais, Paris.

A Moonlight Waltz Suggested by two paintings *Summer Night* by Winslow Homer in the Musée d'Orsay, Paris and *The Lute Player* by Frans Hals in the Louvre, Paris. In the background also was the poem *Sad Strains of a Gay Waltz* by Wallace Stevens and the musical piece *Valse Triste* by Jean Sibelius.

Scallop Maggie Hambling's sculpture *Scallop* celebrates the composer Benjamin Britten and stands on the beach at Aldeburgh, Suffolk. The words "I hear those voices that will not be drowned", a line from Britten's opera Peter Grimes, are cut through the metal of the sculpture.

Shaping Spirit A response to a number of water-and-stone themed paintings by Catriona O'Connor which formed part of an exhibition of her work at St. John's Art Centre in Listowel in April 2019.

The Artist Among the Mountains Suggested by the painting *A Portrait of Ambrogio Raffaele* by John Singer Sargent (Palazzo Pitti, Florence).

Thumb The sources are specified in the poem.

Piper Suggested by a painting by Bob Ó Cathail.

The Piper's Exhalation Written in response to various pieces played by the Galician piper Carlos Nuñez

The Raven's Lamentation Suggested by the old Scottish Gaelic song *Pìobrachd Dhòmhnuill Dhuibh.*

The Hour of the Day Suggested by the painting *Violinist at the Window* by Henri Matisse (Centre Pompidou, Paris).

Workshop The reference behind the poem is *L'Atelier Brancusi,* the gallery recreating the workshop of the sculptor Constantin Brancusi (Centre Pompidou, Paris).

The Art of Belief Suggested by the painting *Saint Dominic* by Cosimo Tura (Uffizi Gallery, Florence).

The Gilt Seahorses of *Nossa Senhora del Rosario* The church in question is in Olhao, Portugal.

Chrysalis Smiles Written after a recital presented as part of the Valentia Chamber Music Festival in August 2018.

Raising the Siege Suggested by an RTÉ National Symphony

Orchestra performance of Shostakovich's *Leningrad Symphony*, conducted by Stanislav Kochanovsky, in the National Concert Hall in October 2018.

A Poet in Bronze Written in a café beside a sculpture entitled *Homage to Pessoa* by Jean-Michel Folon in Largo de São Carlos, Lisbon.

The Poem Rescued Suggested by a recording of Gregorio Allegri's *Miserere*, as sung by the Choir of King's College, Cambridge, on the CD *The Renaissance of Italian Music*.

III

Statuesque Written in response to a bronze sculpture by Laurence Edwards at The White House Farm, Great Glemham, Suffolk, UK.

The Sleep of Reason Creates Monsters The poem takes its title from an etching by Francisco Goya. It was also suggested by a card-playing trope from the poem *Cabhair Ní Ghairfead* by Aogán Ó Rathaille.

During Donald Trump's Inauguration On May 18, 1952, Paul Robeson performed an outdoor concert for more than 25,000 people gathered on both sides of the United States/Canadian border at Peace Arch Park in Blaine, Washington State. His passport had been confiscated by the State Department.

In a Walled Garden Written after a number of visits to *Le Mémorial des Martyrs de la Déportation*, a memorial to the 200,000 Jews deported from Vichy France to the Nazi concentration camps during World War II. It is located below ground level behind the Cathedral of Notre Dame on Île de la Cité, Paris.

Dance of the City Written in response to *La Danse* by Henri Matisse (Musée d'Art Moderne de la Ville de Paris).

Badhbh Written in response to the painting *La Guerre (War)* by Henri Rousseau (Musée d'Orsay, Paris). The title is a Gaelic word that combines the meanings of 'carrion crow' and 'war goddess'.

Light Two paintings lie behind this poem: *Guernica* by Pablo

Picasso (Museo Reina Sofía, Madrid) and *The Third of May 1808* by Francisco Goya (Museo del Prado, Madrid).

Piobrachd Written in response to the playing of *Gol na mBan san Ár* by the piper David Power, as played on his CD *The Eighteen Moloney.*

The White Bear Written in response to a sculpture of the same name by François Pompon (Musée d'Orsay, Paris).

War Pipes Suggested by the legend behind the Scottish Gaelic song *Uamh an Òir,* as sung and played on the CD *Fhuair Mi Pòg* by Margaret Stewart & Allan MacDonald, as well as by the poem of the same name by Somhairle Mac Gill-Eain (Sorley MacLean).

IV

Family Meal Written in response to the painting *Dinner by Lamplight* by Félix Valloton (Musée d'Orsay, Paris).

A Postcard from Knossos Written after a visit to the site of the palace at Knossos, Crete.

Faustina Shivers Written after a conflict between bureaucracy and the arts, a conflict in which everybody lost, including the bureaucracy personnel. I do not wish to be more specific.

Triptych for a Neighbour Suggested by a plaster-cast buddha that overlooks the sea from a small cliff at the end of my garden.

The Bell for Order Suggested by the song *The Castle of Dromore,* as sung by the late Eamon Langford of Kells, Co. Kerry.

Candle Suggested by a paschal candle seen in St. Mark's English Church, Florence.

The Configuration of Love Suggested by sections of the orchestral suite *The Planets,* by Gustav Holst.

A Bracelet from Florence Written to accompany a silver bracelet I bought on the Ponte Vecchio, Florence.

Afternoon Pilgrimage *Santo André de Teixido* is a pilgrimage
village among the cliffs of the coast of Galicia, northwest Spain.

In a Hammock in Galicia Suggested by *An Lebor Gabála*, the
mythological conquest of Ireland by Amergin and the Milesians
from Galicia.

The Place of Prayer Written in response to *Six Prayers*, a tapestry
woven as a Holocaust memorial by Anni Albers, and which
was part of a 2018 exhibition of her work at the Tate Modern
Gallery (London).

Amergin's Ship Written to mark the erection of the bronze
sculpture *Árthach Dána*, by Holger Lönze, in Waterville, Co.
Kerry to mark the landing place of Amergin and the Milesian or
Gaelic people, as related in the mythological *Lebor Gabála*.

Shaping the Place of Speech Written after a talk entitled
Amairgen and Ireland's Myth of Itself, by John Carey, at the 2019
Amergin Solstice Poetry Gathering in Waterville, Co. Kerry.

Dance Written in response to *Carbon, time and space*, a multimedia
installation created in 2017/18 by Karen Hendy while she was
artist-in-residence in Siamsa Tíre, Tralee, Co. Kerry.

The Dispute about the Immaculate Conception Written in
response to a painting of the same name by Carlo Portelli in the
Basilica di Santa Croce, Florence.

Pietà Written in response to a painting by Mícheál Ua Ciarmhaic,
a reproduction of which can be seen in the anthology *Duanaire
Mhaidhcí*, ed. Paddy Bushe (Coiscéim, 2006).

The Road to God Knows Where Written in response to a
painting of the same name by Seán Hardie.

Listener Written in response to *Écoute*, a sculpture by Henri de
Miller beside the Church of St-Eustache in Paris.

Solstice Written after a Midwinter Day reading at the Íochtar
Cua Alignment, a Bronze Age megalithic alignment near
Waterville, Co. Kerry.

Midwinter Sunset, Cill Rialaig A low stone passageway leading to the principal cell in the remains of the Early Medieval monastery at Cill Rialaig on Bolus Head in Co. Kerry was aligned on the setting sun at the midwinter solstice.

Casting Written after a 2018 gathering in Cillín Liath, Co. Kerry, of *Umha Aois*, a group of artists, archaeologists and others interested in exploring the working methods of Bronze Age craftworkers.

Sky Woman Written after several visits to *Femmes en Mouvement*, a 2015 exhibition of paintings by the Japanese artist Aya Takagi at the Université Paris Descartes exhibition centre.

Woman, Moon and Mountain Written in response to a tapestry woven by the artist Lisbeth Mulcahy.

The Piper Abroad Written in response to the piping of Ailean Dòmhnullach (Allan MacDonald), especially but not exclusively in response to *Chrò Chinn t-Sàile*, often known by its first line *Thèid mi dhachaidh/ I will go home*, a song found on the CD *Fhuair Mi Pòg* by Margaret Stewart & Allan MacDonald.

Forging Icarus Written in response to *Large Icarus*, a sculpture by Fritz Koenig which was included in a 2018 exhibition of his work at the Palazzo Pitti, Florence.

First Day in Varnam Written sitting beside the lotus pond at Varnam Homestay, Kerala, India in February 2018.

Turning the Tune Written in response to the guitarist Steve Cooney's playing of *Tabhair Dom do Lámh*, a 17th century composition by the harpist Ruaidhrí Dall Ó Catháin.